GOWER
POEMS

Robert Edward Gurney

Published by
Llyfrau Cambria Books, Wales, United Kingdom.
Cambria Books is the imprint of
Cambria Publishing Ltd.
Discover our other books at: www.cambriabooks.co.uk

To my wife Paddy.

I would like to express my gratitude to my nephew Sam Gurney for his advice with a number of these poems.

Cover illustration: William Gurney

The Poems

The Swallow

There's an unmade road
that runs behind the dunes
between Horton and Port Eynon.

It has puddles, great round puddles
that, to the eyes of a child,
are like the craters on the moon.

A boy, wades through them,
one after another,
contemplating his reflection.

Out of the corner of his eye
he sees a swallow wriggle free
from under the milky mud
and fly up to a fish-eyed moon.

Harvest in Gower

They are cutting the corn
in the Gower Peninsula.

With an acute distraction
combine harvesters
dash down narrow lanes
between fields
and showers.

One time we couldn't get away with this.

Men would edge slowly
towards the middle of the field
wielding their 'zives'.

A rabbit would bolt for cover
into a shrinking island of corn.

Then scythes would be hurled
at the spirit of the harvest,
while sickle-eyed ravens
waited patiently in the trees.

Gates

The image persists
of a good friend I once had
in Port Eynon.

There he is.

The old village blacksmith
on that wooden bench
in his wide straw hat
that hoarded the sun.

He liked to sit and chat
by the dairy's side.

But his eyes always coveted
the wrought-iron gate
of the house across the road.

Then he would pause
and announce with a sigh
that swelled like a song:

"I made that gate."

His eyes would caress
the curves along the top,
his hands imitate
the movement of waves.

And now I read that they have found
the old iron gate
to Dylan's Boathouse.

Cast into the estuary by builders,
it lay deep within the salt-mud
at Laugharne.

That gate I remember.

It was the one I had once opened
with some difficulty
as a child.

It too had curves along the top
and two swirls in the middle
that peeked out like crab's eyes.

It went just now,
at Sotheby's,
for more than just a song.

The House of Light

A tin roof shelters me from the wind
at the end of the world
in this small bay
of Ushuaia.

An old oil drum
serves as barbecue.

As if in joyful applause
the nervous albatross
claps its bill like claves
upon each piece of meat
it snatches from my hand.

Eyeless in the sun,
the lighthouse
surveys me with a bright monotony:
red, white, red.

It reminds me of the cast-iron sentinel
to Whitford Point.

The Book Launch

As a child
I had always wanted to climb into
the Bard's Chair
that had found its way
to Luton Museum.

And now I sit outside the replica
of Dylan's shed
at the Eisteddfod.

Just a few feet away
this year's Bard
is being crowned.

A kindly vicar stops to chat,
then buys a copy of my book.

A wave of applause sweeps
the dust across the ground.

Why do I feel this dark disquiet
that plays about my feet
in Llanelli?

Why has it chosen to
visit me in Llanelli?

Helwick

I often stand atop the cliff
and wonder where the sandbank lies.

They say it casts off
from Port Eynon Point
to beyond Rhossili.

I often try to descry its lethal fish-spine curves
from patterns in the waves.

A villager from Horton
who claimed he'd Viking blood
told me a man once fished
a horse-shoe from above the Helwick
Bank.

He said that men had seen
the outlines of roads
transcribed upon the sands.

We will probably now never know
whether there ever was a village down there,
as they are dredging once again,
removing the sand for a motorway.

Lyonesse

I have often stood in the wind
at Rhossili
and looked out towards
the Isles of Scilly
lying below the horizon.

I have often wondered
whether the kingdom called Lyonesse
ever existed.

I have often tried to imagine
the roofs, the walls, the belfries,
the casement windows,
the sculpted porches
and the marble flowers
of De la Mare's poem.

Patagonia 8000 Miles

There used to be a sign out there,
on the Worm,
near the Look-Out Station.

It was made of wood,
and was shaped
like a long, squashed hand.

Its giant finger
pointed down
the Bristol Channel.

It said, Patagonia 8000 miles.

No-one seems to know
who has it now, or at least,
that's what they are saying.

Ynys Lanwol

Inverted when we saw it,
the votive offering to Ganesh,
the elephant-god of auspicious starts.

She was surprised
when I reached down
and turned it over.

It was traditional, she said,
to cast an effigy into the water
upon the Feast Day of a God.

I handed it to her
and we continued with our walk
to Burry Holms, restored.

The Beach

Today the water has retreated so far
that the beach resembles a desert.

In the distance lies Burry Holms,
the Hermit Saint Cenydd's tiny isle,
dark, flat, recumbent,
like a toppled statue,
half-submerged.

And here lies the body of a cliff-fallen pony,
its fetlocks feathering
in the tide-combed sand.

Beyond, a gannet's bones,
a dead dolphin,
a pink bottle, plastic doll;
the springs of an old mattress,
the skeleton of an umbrella,
a carved voodoo cuttlefish-bone,
and an elephant-trunked icon,
Ganesh, Hindu God of Beginnings,
whose head once bounced
in the dry Indian sand.

A Lady from Buganda

"Our crickets in Buganda,"
she said, in the car park
by The Vile, in Rhossili,
"are larger than these."

She removed one
from her windscreen
with her finger.

"We used to eat them grilled,
in the City Bar in Kampala.

For many, *nsenene,* as we call them,
are a form of money.

A bagful can buy you a *gomasi,*
the long dress we Baganda women
like to wear.

Our women used not eat them,
for fear of bearing a child
with a head like a cricket.

15

Today, however,
in the outlying villages,
most women do."

I smiled and I nodded.

The Lost Graveyard

I don't know if Dylan saw
bones sticking out of the ground
in the lost village at the bottom
of the cliff in Rhossili.

I don't know if he knew
that Saint Sili's church
may be buried down there,
under the sand.

When reading 'We Lying by Seasand'
I sometimes think that he did.

A Dog with a Bone

Every tile seemed to rattle
with the gasp of breath
that greeted the boy
racing up the road
with the news that the dog
running proudly around the village's streets
had ripped the bone between its jaws
from a bulge in the wall
of the heaving graveyard.

Butterflies

There's a special place
in Port Eynon,
we called it the secret path.

There's a kissing gate
at the end of it,
to stop wild horses
from entering.

In summer the bushes
were filled with butterflies.

The males were bright orange,
the females were pale.

You had to look hard
to see them,
for the light down there
was poor.

But each one,
when you found it,
was like a pointillist painting.

The Witch of Castle Head

There was a bad witch
who got all snarled up
on the rusty barbed wire
at Castle Head in Rhossili.

Her cloak waved in the wind
on the old sagging fence.

Black rags, a pointed hat,
a broom of twigs,
and a head sunk into shoulders
could all be clearly seen.

She took off one day in a howling gale
when driving rain and rattling hail
stung both our eyes and our ears.

It wasn't really a witch, they say,
just an old plastic bag.

The Lady of the Lake

I had a post today
from a friend
on Facebook.

It was of a lady by a lake,
with a mansion
in the background.

Suddenly she morphed into a falcon
and flew towards me.

The Peregrine Falcon

My mind keeps going back
to the bird that burst into my life
that day in Port Eynon.

She was so close,
I could almost reach out
and touch her.

The chevrons on her breast
were like the waves
that children like to draw.

She just sat there on the fence,
staring at me, without blinking,
while I stared back at her.

Dylan Dying

The whole of South Wales
seemed to be burning
that evening, Guy Fawkes.

Columns of black smoke
rose here and there
on the outskirts of Swansea.

I thought I glimpsed Dylan
through a dark curtain.

I saw him for an instant,
struggling for breath,
in a hotel room
in New York.

Dancing on the Down

I can't remember now
where I first heard it,
I don't really know
if it's true.

Someone told me,
many years ago,
that the villagers in Rhossili
used to dance wildly
around a fire on the hillside,
chanting strange incantations.

The flames, he said,
seemed to come
from inside the earth.

It all happened, he said,
before the Reformation.

Dreaming on Rhossili Down

I fell asleep
on top of Rhossili Down
and dreamed of a city
built, not of stone,
but of diamonds and pearls.

The streets were paved with gold
and silver.

It was on an island
but there were no boats.

It was always hidden
under a mist.

Its trees were full of fruit
that gave health and eternal life.

Nobody was born there
and nobody died.

They lived for ever.

Its streets were so wide
that it took a day to cross them.

The church had a bell that,
if it were to have been rung,
could have been heard
all over the world.

It was so large
it would have covered two houses.

On Good Friday, they said,
the domes of the church, its silver cross
and the silver and gold rooftops of the houses
would emerge from the mist.

The people were always happy,
never ill, never hungry, never poor.

They didn't have to work.

And they said, in my dream,
that when you entered,
you forgot how you had got there
and even who you had been.

Time did not exist.

They said
that if you left the city,
you would start to die.

Then I dreamed
that I was walking through fog,
when I saw my father
just as he was,
eleven years ago,
before he died.

'Who are you?' he asked.
'I'm your son', I said.
'You've changed', he said
and he threw his arms
around me.

He then began to change,
going grey and gaunt,
and then he disappeared
in a cloud of dust.

They say that one day
the bell will ring throughout the world
announcing the coming
of the Day of Judgement.

And that then
the City of the Caesars
will be visible for ever.

Not just on Good Fridays.

Moor Ghosts

I have been told
that on a dark night
there, where Dylan finally wanted to live,
on the slopes of Rhossili Down,
below the Moor,
you can sometimes glimpse
the ghosts and the bones
of Stone Age men
coming down
like zombies
towards you.

Pont-y-Cob

I was parked by Pont-y-Cob,
near where the Lliw
joins the Loughor River,
reading *Délie,* by Maurice Scève,
a poet who wrote where two rivers meet,
in Lyons,
when a letter came from a friend
who writes where two rivers meet
and another begins,
in Cipolletti,
Patagonia.

The Minister's Daughter

We were in the car park
of Singleton Hospital
by Swansea Bay.

She was a minister's daughter
from somewhere in Gower.

We had been visiting a lady
who had just had a stroke.

A nun, by her bed, got up and left,
as we went in.

I picked up something,
a small tension between them.

"Don't you like Catholics?" I asked.

"Well, you know," she replied.
"they go round knocking on people's doors
at Christmas, trying to sell you raffle tickets."

Beggar's Pit

I sat down
in Beggar's Pit,
near Hangman's Cross,
above Oxwich Marsh,
in the south of the Gower Peninsula.

I remembered
that tree-creepers make holes
and huddle in groups
in the very soft bark
of redwood trees.

I remembered that nocturnal birds,
like nightjars and owls,
take dust-baths in the still-warm earth
of country roads
in Africa.

I remembered
that a handful of Welsh men and women,
copying the local birds in Patagonia,
dug holes in the ground at night

to escape from the cold wind,
as they moved moving inland
from Golfo Nuevo.

As The Crow Flies

We would ask
our Spanish teacher,
Mr Enyr Jones,
how far it was
to Gaiman,
in Patagonia,
where he was born.

His eyes would fill with tears,
the air with his sighs.

"Oh, a vuelo de pájaro,
as the crow flies,
about 8000 miles,"
he would reply.

Eaten by Tides

Eaten by tides,
the ribs of the Helvetia sink,
year after year,
further and further
into the sand
of Rhossili Bay,
while, across the water,
bothered by badgers,
lie Dylan and Caitlin,
in the overspill cemetery
of St Martin's church
in Laugharne.

A Dream

I dreamt that I went
into the Swiss Tavern pub,
in Old Compton Street
in London.

I dreamt that I asked the barmaid
if she had found the script of a play
by Dylan Thomas.

She looked under the counter
and passed me the manuscript
in a tattered old folder.

The Broken Pot

I found a bit of a broken pot,
on a corner, near a wall
in the Orchard in Port Eynon,
there where snakes hide
and people dump
unwanted bulbs.

It was just a piece,
just enough for me to guess
its original shape.

And the thought crossed my mind
of Cerridwen,
the Great Celtic Goddesss of Inspiration,

and the hare of Spring that she pulled
out of her cauldron.

The End of the World

A journey to Rhossili
can leave you
speechless.

It is Wales's Land's End,
its End of the World,
its own Finisterre,
the dark curtain
beyond which
nothing is
certain.

Reticulated Ripples

We were, by then, a long way down
Rhossili beach.

The heat was unbearable.

We only had one bottle of water
between us.

The tide was going out.

Then we saw it appear,
a magical pool.

It was shallow,
no more than a square of sand
covered by a thin film of water.

The wind got up
and blew across this pond
that had been left
by the receding sea.

Gusts swirled
and drove the water
this way and that.

Ripples, travelling in one direction,
clashed with those coming from another.

They created
an amazing, blue mosaic,
an abstract work of art,
as good as any
that Gaudí made.

Wrecking

My mind keeps going back
to the same image.

There is no moon.

A man leads a cow
along a path that I have often trod,
a lantern has been tied
to one of its horns.

I feel a need
to paint this scene:
a cowherd and his cow
in a circle of light
cast by a candle
that is burning brightly
inside the lantern.

It feels peaceful.

Then the farmer bends forward
and pulls his cow into the wind.

Below, the sea is boiling.

It's the contrast that strikes me
between the slow progress of the cow,
with its gently swinging lantern,
and the moaning of the waves,
as they shoot up through the Blow Hole
out on the Head.
You can't see the water
rising like a geyser
but you can hear it groaning.

Then I stop and remember:
this was the Wreckers Coast.

The cow and its swinging lantern
are there to lure ships onto the rocks.

Desperate for the safety of a port,
sailors are seeking the mast-light
of a ship at anchor.

Good men will perish tonight
at the base of the cliff.

Their bodies will be found at dawn.

The whole village will go down
to look for Norwegian timber,
for gold from Spain,
for brandy from France
and a pair of leather shoes.

The Girl on the Edge

I could never understand why
I couldn't finish this book.
I began it years ago
but each time that I felt
that it was complete,
something told me
that it wasn't.

Then, this week,
I finally understood.

A family took their daughter
for a picnic on the cliffs.
She was eighteen months old.
The war had just ended.
Rhossili was no longer off-limits.
The barbed wire had gone,
the Americans too.

With them was a young woman,
a niece, evacuated from London
to their house in Swansea.

It was she who told me.

They laughed about the war,
about how they had sat up in bed,
the three of them, in Sketty,
and put their gas masks on,
when the sirens sounded.

The parents were chatting,
the young child was testing her legs.

She ran at great speed
towards the edge of the cliff.

The young lady's fiancé,
an RAF pilot,
seeing what was happening,
ran as fast as he could
and swept the child up in his arms.

That child on the cliff,
seventy-two years ago,
was my wife
who has just left us.

The Soul

To Paddy

In my Gower room,
an intense golden cloud,
warm and comforting,
like the celestial light
you can come across
when the sun shines
through the mist in Fall Bay,
came down towards me.

It wrapped itself around me,
enveloping me in its love,
leaving me in no doubt,
that, at that very moment,
she was telling me
I should not worry,
that she was safe
and that I would be too.

Other books by the author:

La poesía de Juan Larrea, 1985
Nueve monedas para el barquero,
antología, 2005
Luton Poems, 2005
Poemas a la Patagonia, 2005
El cuarto oscuro y otros poemas, 2008
La libélula y otros poemas / The Dragonfly
and Other Poems, 2012
La casa de empeño y otros poemas / The
Pawn Shop and Other Poems, 2014
A Night in Buganda, 2014
Dylan's Gower, 2014
To Dylan, 2014
Bat Valley, 2017
Absurd Tales fron Africa, 2017
El acantilado y otros poemas, 2017
Antología poética de Robert Gurney, 2018

Translation:
Bohoslavsky, A., *The River and Other*
Poems, 2004

PRAISE FOR THE AUTHOR'S WORK

By Dedwydd Jones

Thank God for Robert Edward Gurney's two volumes of poetry, *To Dylan* and *Dylan's Gower*, the best collection of Welsh verse since RS Thomas. These are short poems like the Japanese haiku or the wonderful Welsh englynion, presenting a world of observation in a few words – as Gurney does – just find the image, fix it, present it and then move on to the next, no messing! And no Dylan imitations either although Gower was Dylan's backyard where poetry positively 'flowed through the air'! The poems too celebrate place names as Dylan himself did so brilliantly.

The collected titles are poetry in themselves: 'Port Eynon from Space', 'On Llanmadoc Hill', 'The Mist', 'Crows' and 'Fires', 'The Tears of St Lawrence', 'The Poundffald', 'Chatterpies', 'The White Lady of Oystermouth Castle', 'Walking the Worm', 'Dylan and the Monster', all set firmly in Gower – the best of Wales for a very long time.

To Dylan and *Dylan's Gower* are an antidote to anyone suffering from the dolorous hiraeth of home, especially the Gower of Cymru.

Thank you ROBERT GURNEY.

Dedwydd Jones, Bedford, England, 8 January 2016.
Dedwydd Jones, playwright, author of the *Black Book On The Welsh Theatre (The Early Years 1947 - 1995)*, Foreword by Jan Morris, Creative Print Publishing Limited, 2012.

www.ingramcontent.com/pod-product-compliance
Lightning Source LLC
Chambersburg PA
CBHW070830100426

42813CB00003B/561